THE

WAY

LAND

BREAKS

THE
WAY
LAND
BREAKS

POEMS

REBECCA BROCK

Sheila-Na-Gig Editions

ISBN: 9798987305843
Library of Congress Control Number: 2023933168

Sheila-Na-Gig Editions
Russell, KY
Hayley Mitchell Haugen, Editor
www.sheilanagigblog.com

ACKNOWLEDGMENTS

Delight and gratitude to the editors and readers of the following journals in which these poems first appeared:

Anti-Heroin Chic: "A Presbyterian Walks into a Crystal Shop," "Tammi Calls From Walmart,"

Bellevue Literary Review: "When Honey Wouldn't Do" (now titled "I Used to Think My Mother Was a Miracle")

CALYX: "My Mother Says She Won't Outlive the Dog"

The Comstock Review: "Sometime in the Late Age of a Long Marriage"

Cutthroat, A Journal of the Arts: "Octopus"

The Dodge: "Bone Collector, Mad Woman, Boy Mom," "Sunlight in Fog"

K'in: "The Story They Are Telling Now"

Literary Mama: "My Mother Suggests a Tranquilizer"

The Orchards Poetry Journal: "Bones," "Fine Lines," "Raising Glaciers"

Pirene's Fountain: "Tiger"

Poetry Virginia: "When People Ask My Mother"

River Heron Review: "I Remember How I Believed"

Rust and Moth: "Rare Sighting"

Sheila-Na-Gig online: "Amanita Phalloides," "Expanse, Immensity, Collapse," "On Becoming the Type of Person Who Yells: Dinner!" "Preop," "We Were Never Made to Be Invincible," "When the Sky Tips"

Sky Island Journal: "What the Mother Can't Say to Her Son at 14"

Susurrus: "A Woman Might Say This Is What Birth Looks Like"

Sweet, A Literary Confection: "The Flight Attendant Looks Back," "To My Father Whose Pitch Has Always Been About Surviving"

West Trestle Review: "After Reading Geohazard Warning Signs at Mt. Rainier"

Yellow Arrow: "Borah Peak Earthquake, 1983," "Watching Mountains"

ANTHOLOGIES:

Ecobloomspaces: Poetry at the Intersection of Social Identity and Place (Iron Oak Press, *West Trade Review*, 2024): "A Geography," "Geologic Unconformity," "I Broke the Way Land Breaks"

Sharing This Delicate Bread (Sheila-Na-Gig Editions, 2022): "Expanse, Immensity, Collapse," "Preop"

The following poems also appear in my chapbook, *Each Bearing Out* (Kelsay Books, 2022): "Expanse, Immensity, Collapse," "Preop," "The Story They Are Telling Now," "Tiger," "What the Mother Can't Say to Her Son at 14"

HONORS

"Amanita Phalloides" won *Sheila-Na-Gig online's* Editor's Choice Award, 2022 and was nominated for a Pushcart Prize and Best of the Net.

"Bones" was an honorable mention in the *2021 International Women's Writing Guild Poetry Contest* at Kelsay Books.

"I Remember How I Believed" was a finalist in *The River Heron Review* Editor's Prize.

"Octopus" was a finalist in the 2021 Joy Harjo Poetry Prize at *Cutthroat, A Journal for the Arts.*

"Preop" won *Shiela-Na-Gig online's* 2021 Spring Poetry Prize and was nominated for a Pushcart Prize and Best of the Net.

"Raising Glaciers" won the 2022 Women's Poetry Prize at Kelsay Books, in participation with The International Women's Writing Guild, and judged by Katie Manning.

"Sometime in the Late Age of a Long Marriage" won first prize in *The Comstock Review's* 2022 Muriel Craft Bailey Memorial Prize, judged by Ellen Bass and was nominated for a Pushcart Prize.

"The Stories They Are Telling Now" was nominated for a Pushcart Prize by Kelsay Books.

"When People Ask My Mother" won 3rd place, Poetry Society of Virginia, Loretta Dunn Hall Memorial Prize, 2019.

Gratitude

Deepest thanks and respect to Hayley Mitchell Haugen—your belief in me early on in my return to writing bolstered me. I admire the way you champion poetry and usher new art into the world through Sheila-Na-Gig.

Thank you to the all the editors who published several of these poems. Thanks especially to *The Comstock Review*, Ellen Bass, Kelsay Books, Karen Kelsay, Katie Manning, *River Heron Review*, Robbin Farr and Judith Lagana for honoring my poems.

So much gratitude to Sandy Coomer, Jen Karetnick and Pat Valdata for your time and generous words. And to Jen Karetnick, again, and Catherine Esposito Prescott for *SWWIM* and all I have learned from reading such fresh, new work.

Thank you to Trudy Hale for the wonder that is The Porches, and Anita Darcel Taylor for your luminous company and your joy.

Several of these poems were hatched in the supportive community of the February Poetry Month Poets. Thanks, especially, to Laura Shovan for giving us all such a gift. And to Ruth Lehrer—for reading my early drafts—it's the best when my poems make you swear.

To my tiny but mighty Poetry Book Club—Sarah Bauer, Jenna Korff, and Mae Lindstrom—each of you sister me with your showing up in the world, and your joy when my poems find their way helps carry me.

To all my dear ones—thank you, thank you for showing up and reading and cheering me on. Liona Burnham, Tammi Matz, Michelle McGregor—I wouldn't be me without each of you. And Heather Elizabeth Feely, your life was so *lived*. I can't believe I'm still here without you.

To my sister, Deborah, my Aunties and my parents, Wendy and Darrel Burbank—thank you for such sustaining love. To my kiddos for FINALLY sleeping in on weekends and for the worlds you show me. Christian, thank you for celebrating my poetry habit, and, especially, for falling for this sad girl, all those years ago. And again, to the good dog Oliver, for your staying company at all the odd hours of my days and nights.

for Momala & Pops, my first loves

Contents

There are yet words that come near to the unsayable,
and, from crumbling stones, a new music
to make a sacred dwelling in a place we cannot own.

Rainer Maria Rilke

Set Me Something Solid

Place me. Set me down
like a jaw unhinging—predator
or mother—let the mouth loose
enough that the cub falters
or the prey falls—finds
its way toward free—
soft grass
on padded paws—a river's edge—and knowing
how to swim
when my mother can't—
offer ledges, nooks
and crannies in a face
of stone—I mean a way
toward climbing—a tree branch
low enough to grab and swing
above teeth snap and crunch.
Ascend, repel, recollect—
you see I am frightened
of forgetting—
of what it means
to forget—a healer says
we must walk as if we don't know,
to not name each thing,
as we know it—as you know it—
but already I am a blur,
as I've told you,
I am a mere fraction
of moving light, already
I am born and bone.

On the Tongue

Anyone who knows the desert
or any stretch
of unbearable wild
knows that arch
of sound
like an echo
of our own bones
beyond all vowel
and consonant,
beyond cry or croon
or lullaby:
throat thrown back,
snout skyward,
jaws wide keening—
there is much to suffer.
It is constant as change
to seek a language
that cuts through
our inadequate tongues,
that gets at the thing
that can't be said,
a thing beyond shriek
but containing it,
that salt taste, that acrimony
on the tongue.

A Woman Might Say This Is What Birth Looks Like

Maybe the creek rising,
maybe her skirt in knots,
maybe the current a push
and pull in the same direction,
something she fights
without knowing
until her toes scrabble for purchase,
until her thighs get wet
until staying upright isn't a given
and she knows enough to falter.
The knee is a tender thing:
taking one, falling to, brought to, bending—
she knows the river
that push
of horizon, she knows
her own going.
Life and new life wanting
shield, wanting shelter, wanting
turn, or return. Swollen
breaths like sharp stones—
tongue torn
by her own teeth,
hurt that hurts after
for so long—
there is no cresting
just that rush,
that sink, her body
a beast
knowing shudder,
knowing heave.

Tiger

When I found myself mother
to a boy who would be
interested in tigers,
if there were any
nearby enough to catch,
I began to look for crevices and cracks,
the deep falls, sudden
implausibilities, like a boy's tiger trap:
meat just out of reach,
the whisper sound
of padded paws on leaves
without ground beneath them—
that *whoosh*
of disappearance
that fearful maw
that shaky disbelief
not unlike when there is a baby new,
born, he and I still trembling, still wet,
the orientation—
happens in a moment—
for a tiger, maybe,
but I floundered, there,
at the changes
at the loss—caught
by how little I knew
of tigers, or falls, or
the possibilities
of little boys.

Some Small Other

You break the surface
of the water, you
still small enough
to laugh, to know to laugh,
to not fear it, to squeal
in that first gasp
at the unexpected splash
and drench—you sit safe enough
in your own body,
in your small world
and know it for joy—
new teeth shining,
baby curls dripping—
what a gift you are
in a way you will not know,
until you are the one
loving some small other
of you but not you,
watching this glee—
knowing love like water
finds its way through air and sunlight,
over skin and hair and forehead
like baptism, like play, like a kiss
and a promise
that it will all be
beautiful.

Amanita Phalloides

The mushroom, white, stunning
and suddenly there, near our house, in a town,
between the 7-11 and the vet clinic,
not out in the dark woods, not even down
by the creek that sometimes broke its banks—just there,
by where we were always walking—
a bulbous umbrella, waiting
like a Cheshire cat or a caterpillar
with a face—the boys at that age
of chub and wonder—I used my phone
to catch what I could: their curious heads bending low
just above the wide dome of its rounded top,
that landlocked jellyfish afloat, air instead of saline—
my youngest reached out and picked it—I remember wincing
at the brokenness—things were always
breaking those days, they didn't *walk*
anywhere but ran and crashed and hollered—
so often I couldn't put things back
into any sort of order—I wish now I'd let more be
and I must have wished that a little then, too
because I asked him to show me
and his brother turned to help him hold it—
its head too big now its stalk was snapped,
wobbling the way their heads did not so long ago
when I carried them everywhere
and then I heard the neighbor,
hands pocketed, head at a tilt ask, "Whatcha got there?"
He was so calm. A naturalist
who knew the names of things.
What is it called I asked or might have
but he said to go ahead and put it down
to have the children wash their hands
maybe even change their clothes,
he spoke slow to me, and gently,

and so I didn't jump at first,
it dawned slowly, and then I moved
the way mothers do.

Bone Collector, Mad Woman, Boy Mom

My youngest son,
who could always fit through
when and where
you were not supposed to,
found a squirrel, sleeping, he said;
knowing better
I had to kneel
to see and wanted to say
yes, yes just sleeping.
A side sleeper, even—look
at the haunch of his shoulder
and hip, the way his tail
stretches peaceful—
Let him be, we said.
And then winter long enough
to rearrange more than a few things.
But the squirrel remained,
wouldn't have, probably,
if the bigger kids knew about it
but he got home midday
back then and something
reminded him to check
or maybe just the scent of earth
led him to the bones:
the tiny knee cap, the shoulder—
he stayed with the body
and I walked back home
to get a container—saying to myself: *bone collector,*
mad woman, boy mom.
The skull with its emptiness
the tally of ribs and teeth—
part of why I grabbed a container,
agreed to it, was that we had to leave—
take the dog to see the vet

where my son told her
about his squirrel
and she asked to see—
put on gloves,
spread out cloth,
laid each small relic—
we were only missing
a few toes, phalanges—
she corrected, a child again
but with the names for things—
clavicle, scapula, patella—and oh—
that intact tail. My son
leaned toward her litany,
repeating, almost a gathering
of two souls, three—
I know I'm a little too quick to hunger
for beauty
but it felt like holy prayer, it did,
all that wonder
between them.

Expanse, Immensity, Collapse

When did time start? my son asks, looming at 4 am.
The animal in me startles, cries out—
his face so close and sudden in the dark,
it's only a moment that I don't know him.
But it's the kind of thing he asks.
He could mean the tick of the clock,
his knowledge of bedtime, time to wake up,
or he could mean his own beginning.
Burdened with a restless mother,
he understands distance is a thing to measure
(how much longer mama?)
between here and there and when
we are on our way toward home again.
Already he's unearthed stories of stone fish
in a Wyoming desert, of cliffs in Nova Scotia
scored with prehistoric trees, an Oreodont skull
in South Dakota—he knows that rocks themselves have ages.
He might have been asking about old human things:
temple gods and sacred rites, lost cities—
he's raced his brother around ancient mounds in Ohio,
walked undulations of an earthen serpent's
twists and turns once aligned with moon, sun,
and steady seeming stars.
Do you hear that? he asks after I've coaxed him
back beneath the covers, snuggled down
beside him—a sound like clanging pipes,
like a radiator we don't have, shudders
and I rise to look out the window,
turn to tell him it is only hard rain.
There are at least two ways
to measure a life: the human one,
and the universe's grander score
of expanse, immensity, collapse.
I lie awake to the wash of it.

The Flight Attendant Looks Back

Even though you arrive,
you're never quite home.
Life lands unexpected.
Here, rain looms heavy,
days thick with leftover wet,
sudden deluge—you miss
not how the rain falls,
or how it smells,
but how you could see it fall,
from what distance—
you know you went too far, wanting
departure, connection—
a certain way of smiling, you left
expecting too much, you recall
now the scent of rain
on dry earth, a storm,
well ahead, above an open stretch
of high desert,
how sometimes rain evaporates
before it reaches ground.

When People Ask My Mother

When people ask my mother
how many children she has, she hesitates.
From a place among others,
also waiting,
I watched my older sister
form and form and form
from mere mass into shape—
into something:
a light lit hand
an unblinking eye
as if she really were my sister known
and lost
before I was capable of knowing.

I must have watched my mother too,
before, even, she felt my kick
and flutter and knew
not to trust it.

Borah Peak Earthquake, 1983

They didn't mean to frighten me.
I was eight and thought my thick-lensed
pink-rimmed glasses
had gone off—the earth,
solid, but also liquid,
the grown-ups at a loss.
Our parents already at work,
my little sister and I at the neighbor's—
the man hollering at us to get outside,
the woman shouting to stay
because the ground might open wide,
might swallow us—and I saw
how their driveway would crack
like a prehistoric egg of soil and stone.
"Again," my sister called, "again,"
thinking it fun, the ride of it, the shake
the earth was giving us—
like a horse losing patience
with the bridle or the buzzing
bodies of the flies.
I didn't know, then,
how it always feels
like that when you are grown—
the push to stay and shelter in place
or the pull to venture out,
to take the risk of street, and sky—
all along your indecision
the solidness of things shifting.

I Used to Think My Mother Was a Miracle

Her smile pretty, without lipstick,
and my father—his face falling
back to normal from the deep lines—
the way he'd hold her against him,
like something without bones
and say, *damn you.*
It was always surprising us,
happening in the middle of a movie,
or just after dinner. Her sugar's plummet
my father's call for juice or honey.
We didn't always have to go
to the hospital in the middle
of the night in our pajamas.
But sometimes she'd clamp her lips,
like a child refusing.
I used to wonder where she went,
how far away a person can be
from someone else.
When her sugar came up enough
she'd look at us like we were brand new
pennies, shining there, for her:
Oh, hi sweethearts, I didn't know
you were all here.
And then, we'd barely stop
to wipe our eyes or breathe
or figure out what we had to do next.
Even Dad would start to crease
around his eyes. We were like people
in a movie when the car
almost drives off a cliff—
for a little while, beneath us,
we'd felt air instead of ground.

A Geography

I tell my sons that sometimes the land shifts.
The creature of it rising
on one shoulder, regardless
of how solid
it once seemed.

Each summer, I drive them
through land they didn't grow up in—
far enough West my eyes snag
on fault lines, trace my own
rough edged, raised up scars
like a tongue tracing teeth—
a step into air
I thought was ground.

My grandfather called them *scarp*—
these old land wounds—
I thought he'd made the word up
like how he called me Squidunk
and my sister, Pipsqueak.

Years and years he sold typewriters
out of his car, through Montana, Wyoming,
Utah, Idaho. Wide plains and then dark rock
here and there like cliffs, a river
snaked like its name
clear through, hills—
all jumbled haunches,
mounded shoulders, giving way
to rocky edges and, closer to the road,
rock spine stacked—
maybe the Lost River Fault
or the Sawtooth or the Big Flat

or just some unnamed stretch of earth
where it once faltered.

My grandfather, his actual end,
took 10 solid days.
His hands, stammering
on the end of stick-like arms.
At the very last, he extended
his right hand to his wife
of 64 years and introduced himself.

It was only a summer or two ago
I learned *escarpment*:
a line of cliffs, formed by a faulting,
or a fracturing, of the earth's crust.
Or, more simply, *scarp*—
not a made-up word
but one which plays close friends with scrap
as in scrap of land or scrappy,
another word for determined,
like my grandfather, my sons, me—
this is land language
meaning rock, meaning exposed fault line,
meaning the land rose up
and there, just there—
you can see how big the shift was.

My Son Says We Have No Culture

Mako Sica: Badlands Nat'l Park

I never expect stone to change
as I watch, but light shifts
the face of it: purple moment
to blue-edged daylight,
the air already talking,
full of dove
and Western Meadowlark.
The Juniper holds movement like gold,
a child's hand playing the wind.
We didn't stay long
at Mount Rushmore.
We took a quick picture
but the heads were big
and so beyond us—
it's hard to get the whole of anything.
I admit I feel some pull
to Scottish crosses, some old echo
passed down my blood
as a whisper of holy.
But it's this land—reduced
to bones: ochre, pale gray,
burnt red—that places me
on this wide earth: the vast plain,
the unhinged open sky,
the roil of grass
that used to hold sea.

Beasts

We'd all wanted to see bison—that roam
we'd seen pictured in the gift shop
at the visitor center. *We might not see a thing,*
we'd said, but still we chose to go—out of our way,
off our careful itinerary—adding hours
to our day and drive. We drove sleepy
through the Black Hills and, less than a mile
from the park exit, there was no sign
of bison at all. We are good at trying,
my husband and I, to make the best
of what's handed us—and so we pulled
the van over to gaze at the village life
of prairie dogs, found only in North America,
we said, look, how that one nuzzles, that one romps—
how they disappear—that quiver and scurry,
the fat little bellies and impossible small hands—
the boys—unplugged enough to marvel
did so, or we thought they did—
but then a blonde in a dark suburban
skidded gravel and hollered her drawl
toward us—*hey y'all, there's buffalo just around the bend.*
And so we scurried to seatbelt and car start,
waving our thanks—it was a moment
from where we'd been, that roam of dark hides,
those creatures, half beast, their soft wet elephant eyes—
they were a traffic jam, their rumps naked
like supersized wildebeest. The bull's head
eclipsed the whole of our windshield
and from the back seat my youngest
breathed, *Oh, hello, you beautiful beasts*—
and all the planning and the packing and the whining
and the driving and the trying—exploded
out my chest, like a bird that didn't even know
she'd been caught, sudden catching sky.

Geologic Unconformity

This mountain, this erosion
of a mountain—against my palm
the warm stone arcs
like a dollar store puzzle
that fits, but barely holds—
I ask my son, *What was it?*
It meant absence, it meant gap—
He sighs from the depths
of his new voice, recalls the park ranger
from yesterday: *Geologic Unconformity, Mom.*
And I remember how it felt
like something I already knew—
that record of no record:
an accounting of absence
equal to years. Millions,
more by millions than we
have even been wandering here.

This is the year I watch
my son's shoulders gain even height
with mine. Silver strands of hair,
among my brown recall
my grandfather, his auburn hair
and how it turned white
over the course of one night.
How this is told as some measure
of his immeasurable loss, his gap
between times: one night,
a young enough man
went to sleep, and when he woke
he was old.

I don't know what happens to a person
between one thing and the next,

how it holds through bones—beneath skin,
a striated measure of when
and how the heart gives out
or how it changes cadence,
changes shape—here:
a grandfather and the boy
he never met who carries his name,
and a woman, suddenly me,
letting go strands to glint
and tangle stone, or wind—
all of it telling
how not one of us
can stay.

What the Mother Can't Say to Her Son at 14

We used to watch cloudscape
unfurling like timelapse,
the sky shifting an exhale
past the Missouri River,
heading West, chasing
the dry breeze, pushing
you ahead of me—or pulling you
behind, you and me, not yet bones, ajar
of what is, what was, what shall be.
I can't tell you how it comes,
caused by implications of the sun
from east or west, this wind
shifts light, changes the face
of stone, tells as many tales
as any stationary thing.
It takes my own breath in gusts,
in fists unseen, in tangle and toss
across the distance of motion, rise,
force and torrent—I see you
surrounded, free, ruddy cheeked,
your hat taking off—
everything that wants to
could fly for a while,
could glide thermals
like a full bellied hawk
with time to spend
on pleasure, even a blade
of grass can sing like a scream—
leave us wondering
what spirit, what worn away thing,
holy or otherwise,
just passed by,
leaving you gleaming.

Marshmallows

after "Cotton Candy" by Edward Hirsch

We set up camp at the base of the Sawtooths,
near where my grandfather once loved to fish,
and my sons ate marshmallows, toasted warm,
saving the burnt ones for their grandmother,
a diabetic, who shouldn't have eaten one
but ate three with great praise, savoring
the residue on her fingers and the grin
of my youngest who says he is a chef
and begged her to eat just one more.
I don't even like marshmallows
but found myself eating one
just because mountains and starlight and campfire
and my father, my mother—my boys, all here—
the way they look at her—and she them—
is still an unexpected thing and I know the mountains
rise up behind us and a coyote howls far off
and in the morning we will take the boys
out onto the lake that was once red with salmon,
that is named, still, for those salmon
and we will find things to do that are easy,
that let her sit still or walk only a few steps
down to the dock, onto the boat—and she will radiate
that sweetness that is her secret. My boys—
bigger now, and busy, constant—
will nestle in beside her and find stillness,
find home—the sweet will kill her, her body
undoing itself, but she won't disappoint them.
One more, she will say, *just one more.*

I Remember How I Believed

For so long I imagined life
a before and after
of some terrible disaster
as if that's how I would be defined:
I was this and, now, I'm that.
A sometimes Presbyterian raised among Mormons,
a family of Jehovah's Witness next door—
always the end of times, always something coming:
grasshoppers & heat & days of summer
time turning weeks turning years I couldn't stop,
my mother sick all through,
her first baby buried
in the foothills under a Western white pine.
As a child I imagined I could crawl
into those foothills—beast creatures,
sleeping old ancient—turn around twice
between hill rise, and settle,
nose to tail, tucked
against that pale brown rise—
there—even grown I half want
to see it wake. The wind quicks
as if it knows what I want
and don't want. Every June
I watched my father
clear the baby's headstone
with water from the cemetery pump,
he traced the cursive O of *Our*,
the D of *Darling* and I remember
how I believed that line
would be solid between then
and now, what was
and what now will be.
Sometimes after driving for days,
or hiking for hours, the distance

a being stretched between here
and home, I can't tell
which one of us
is breathing.

After Reading Geohazard Warning Signs at Mt. Rainier
for Liona

I learn the word *lahar*: mudflow, landslide,
that rushed obliteration of pyroclastic flow,
also that volcanos have flanks,
and the river is the thing to watch—does it rise?
Move quickly, the signs say, *to higher ground*.
Someday, the mountain might remember what it is.
My friend understands. It is her mountain.
Ours, she calls it, referencing her daughters,
her husband, her local friends—the life she's built,
within sight of it. *On clear days*
you can go far and still see it, she says.
But it stays hidden from me,
mist and cloud and trees obscuring
as though what is there, isn't.
She says it's sad when the mountain
doesn't come out, as though it were a child.
I tell her how, once, in Japan, I stood
on a train platform, Mount Fuji loomed
over everything and I heard sound
that was more a disturbance of sound,
a shift in air molecules, in my molecules—
by the time I turned, the bullet train
was a going blur my husband never even saw—
Shinkansen, he breathed through the reverberation.
If I had leaned out, even a little—
I'd have gone with it.
My friend knows how much I need
the names of things, as if to name is to know,
to see it coming. She says they have a plan,
a meeting place—*the girls know*
where to go, she says, *and the cats,*
the cats are smart. Maybe the sound.

Maybe the change in the air.
Maybe how sometimes water rises
as if inevitable, as if there is no other way
for water to be but rising.

My Mother Says She Won't Outlive the Dog

Says she doesn't want to.
We are turning left on Franklin
a nothing road in my nothing town—
I don't live here anymore but she does
so she's the one driving, and I'm the one looking
beyond the streets and houses and chain stores,
to the mountains and the hills, the sky that pulls down differently
and she says she read that if you are overweight
and over 70, drink wine & coffee,
you will live longer.
"Well, shit," she says and
I think maybe I should be the one driving the car.
My own heart beat
neither wants nor doesn't want to live.
It just does.
At the stoplight she doesn't see
the birds pulse the air, that beat of wings.
the swoop, and rise.
I would like to ask my mother how they know
the when and where
of expanse and collapse.
I roll down the window to hear her
say it will mess up her hair,
but the birds are calling, anyway,
the leaves falling, anyway,
the people you love leaving, anyway,
or staying when you go—

Rove: The Flight Attendant Considers Opportunity

From the sky, the land looks comprehensible,
even at night—all the clustered lights,
even the moon on dark water.
The airplane climbs and I whisper
rehearsed commands: *heads down,*
stay down, release seat belts,
leave everything, cross your arms—
jump. The groan and pulse
of a 737, familiar
as my own belly noises.

On Mars, Opportunity goes dark.
My sister's text comes through when I land
in Tucson—the Rover's last words:
my battery is low and it's getting dark.
The other flight attendant jokes
her last words will be a sparkling:
"Good morning, welcome aboard!"

Yesterday I was in Virginia,
saw the sun set in California,
watched it rise this morning in Arizona,
opened curtains to mountains
I didn't even know
were there. I knew the trees
were trees but not their names,
the birds were birds, quick,
and dark, but not familiar
like that muffled roar,
that sound of highway,
like my childhood home
which is to say kind of lonely
with an awareness of others

leaving or heading out beyond
just now.

Imagine roving that long
and that wide under space sky,
alone on another rock
that maybe once was
with valley and hill,
tides of sand: *there is this, there is this* —
and, without saying, there is also me:
diligence or curiosity
programmed to rove and see.

I didn't mean to go so far,
I could say this to my mother.
When my sons were little
I left notes and a magnet map
of this country, the states
all in a pile, a list
of where I'd be and not be
when I was gone.

Home, I wash off the smell
of airplane, sort laundry, start dinner,
help my youngest with his homework.
He asks how to spell *opportunity* —
he is the one who wants to fly,
to spend life with different tethers,
watching lights become sudden,
watching ground
become close.

What to Tell Them

When it gets full dark,
my youngest says,
we are going to lay on the ground
and look for constellations.
Missing two teeth, he says it crooked,
the *t* a disappearance, so I hear: *consolations.*

I am checking in, on orbit
from my older son's baseball game.
I watch when he is catching,
or up at bat, and then loop to find
the tagalongs, younger siblings
running free—the little girl
with hair like sunlight,
shows me a thick black cricket
and says, *He is so sad.*

But the cricket looks like a cricket.
Not unhappy or happy.
Its feelers wave gently.
My son, his hair tufting out at odd angles
from a too short haircut, asks earnestly
for a blanket, and money
for popcorn, or hot chocolate,
he tries to say, *I think that star is actually Saturn.*
The cricket chirps.
It means, the little girl explains,
I love you and good luck.

It is early in October and they don't know
about yesterday—how gunfire exploded
into and through a crowd
of human beings.
They don't know yet

how surprising it is
to not feel
surprised.

But I am a child
of this planet, too.
I don't tell them I am playing my life
beside the bigger game
I don't want to play
but vaguely understand.

A foul ball flies and all the parents
yell, at once, *heads up!*

I get a blanket from the car,
buy them popcorn
and hot chocolate
from the concession stand.
I point out some stars, a planet—
I listen with admiration
to the cricket.

Preop

The surgery room, after the bustle and baby talk
of the prep, is a bright unremarkable surprise.
Also cold. Masks and hats looming. The old look older,
I assume, because I know the small look smaller,
the vulnerable—well, I am only allowed back
because I am the mother and the medical staff
are doing camaraderie, the wink and the nudge
and the friendly, friendly fire before the undoing,
before repairing the undone. It is hard for me
to act as though it is not hard to be alive—
my boy is stiff and terrified and breathing quick,
willing himself to hold, to stay still.
Even still, he grimaces at the anesthesia mask,
and I reach to help hold it—
Well aren't you useful, mom, someone says.
I mumble something back but that's the whole of me—there—
holding the mask and he's trying not to go under,
his eyes trying to open up against their closing,
he pants *into* the mask—fighting—
and I'm telling him—this child, this boy
whom I've taught everything from look both ways,
to pedal, pedal, pedal, to c-a-t cat, to 1 plus 1,
to wash your hands, brush your teeth, wash
your parts, don't hug your friends so hard,
say please, say thank you, look people in the eye
when you speak— *breathe, buddy, just breathe*—
he fights until it seizes him,
the easy drift a hard crash.
I say what all the mothers must say: *he's really special*
and find myself making pleading prayer hands,
please and thank you and God bless hands—
two of the nurses can't meet my eyes,
one is crying, maybe other mothers
are tougher or maybe nurses

understand, more than most,
or maybe it was just him,
that last fight he gave before going out,
that spirit: its pulse and serve,
its oddity and fight.

Bloodwork

It's easy to get a draw on me.
Make a fist, they say weakly
but I'm never sure they mean it.
They've never missed.
My vein opens willingly, offering up
as much as is needed, every time.
Still, I look away for a moment
as if that changes things, and think
about the folds of the brain, the muscles
binding joints—how even the X-ray
shows mostly shadows
around bone, how the MRI
can come back so clear
as if internally I am obvious,
a sort of machine that began with a ball
dropping
on a lever that released
more balls or a shoe
on a stick that kicked a drum
whose vibration let loose
a weighted string—triggered
a coil of spring, tipped a bucket
of bright paint, from some height—
actions, large and small and necessary,
to the whole motion
of happening, moving, inexorably
to some finale—
quiet or otherwise—
the end, no matter
the spectacle, or lack of it—
a sort of letting down, obvious
all along now, how that weighted ball
might unsettle, nudge
off course—we, none of us,
without variables.

My Mother Suggests a Tranquilizer

And I think of beasts—
that strange shift in a wild eye
toward absence—an elephant's knees
in collapse, the lion's mane
matted from the muzzle, or the rhinoceros
tied, dangling, by her feet
from a helicopter.

My mother insists on gladness,
a Disney princess mother who actually kept
a wild squirrel for a pet, birds came to her—
on purpose. I was her shadow,
shirking her lightness, her ease, her aim
all these years, her intention, even now,
to pull me down, make the bed soft,
the days bright, happiness
the rule of law and land.

Sometimes my son looks at me
the way an animal would—
quick and caught—
and I say, *babe,*
everything isn't meant to be okay—
just to see the boy in him
shift, and settle, know his sorrow,
name it human,
even necessary.

Shadows and Tall Trees

Sometimes the wind kicks up
and feels like urging—otherwise
I don't think about her much, my shadow
trailing behind me, treading
in the background of my trudge—
on and on, she must think, *all that walking*
and stopping—she must wonder why
I make her look up at tall trees
or maybe she knows, says *hello*
in her own way to the trees I visit.
Maybe they say to each other, the tree's shadow
and mine—*there they go again,*
those two, mooning at each other's lines
in broad daylight
as if there's not eight billion people
and 400 billion trees
with sun all bright between them,
all that sky above—
I must be such a disappointment
to her, my staid middle age
riddled with a sloppy stack
of autoimmune the doctor likes to call "my soup."
I've only ever liked soup, really,
for the warm bread that comes with it—
maybe she was whispering all along:
lay off the bread, lighten up.
Maybe she is where my light went
for that long stretch—the hard one
when I had such trouble with the hours
in a day—my son choosing
that time or time just choosing him—
to move out from boyhood,
to leave me here,
behind his shadow,

watching, wondering at him
the way I do with my trees
that aren't even mine
except that I know them,
the way light plays, the way shadow falls
on limbs, the way they look full,
and emptied—the way they stand
wind and rain, or wait for snow,
the grace there is in crooked lines—
tree roots, branches, hairy legs
and sudden big feet—
his shadow towering
over mine.

Fine Lines

after Brené Brown

She reads that midlife is when the universe
puts its hands on you, draws you close
and says: *listen, I'm not fucking around.*
So she resets her shoulders,
squares them down her back,
and reminds herself without saying
to stand up straight.
Days feel tumultuous
and full of moment, that awareness of brevity
makes her begin to watch the sky —
to look up more, to see the path itself,
even the way it turns. Walking the dog
becomes an excuse
for walking the self.
Something always hurts,
sometimes a shoulder, sometimes a back, or a hip —
sometimes the brain as though weighted
as though shaded with loss and bewilderment
and sometimes the heart —
beats get noticed, the breaths
prodded by the mind
as deep ins and outs.
She's learned it's normal to feel despair
at this or any age. Also rage.
After all she is doing the impossible.
Anybody that's paying attention knows
about upkeep and loss, the constant roil
and change of the body, the heart.

My Mother as the Sun

She is breathless because her lungs always falter,
her gait tipping off balance because her body
still imagines herself a small woman,
feet shaped for high heels—*no one would believe
I used to be kinda cute,* she says to the mirror.
I say she's beautiful and she doesn't believe it—
just as I never believed her all those years
looking or forgetting to look at the sun of her.
Vera Bradley is having a sale, but before
I can ask: *is it the navy blue you want?*
and before she can say: *turquoise,*
with purple and white—her sugar plummets—
we find a candy bar in her old purse,
hot pink and purple floral,
and sit on a curb because the bench
isn't in the shade and there's a hot flash
coming on in me. She says, *there's a fan, in the purse.*
Her Snickers going slow, we swelter,
shade our eyes with our hands, know
we should look for better shelter,
or an answer to the blood sugar
that's faltering, all the time, lately. *Good grief,*
she says, *aren't we a picture.*
But I can still see how she was made
to laugh and maybe spin, and dance—
her not wanting me to know the words
for sorrow so much that it seems to be
the only language I ever really learned
to listen for—how heavy
I must have been, must be, to bear—
and so, I tilt the fan like a courtesan,
turn myself proper British,
drawl: *such fun,* and it's instant, easy
to let our eyes start with tears,

and then laughter—at how women burn,
at floral print purses, the revelation
of the usefulness of painted paper fans
and old candy bars—she takes the next bite
with her pinky finger raised
as if her very fine grandmother
wouldn't be abhorred at our chaos,
our curb squat, our girth and bulk and heat—
and we're off again, not on earth at all,
chortling and gathering looks
from other still wandering stars
lingering unseen
because of the sunlight,
because of my mother's brightness
because I never do trust
light to last.

Sunlight in Fog

The goose, swooping low and sudden
over my roof, expected to land on water,
but belly-skidded across asphalt
before righting himself
and gazing down his bill
for a measured moment.

I could almost hear him clear his throat
and mutter *nothing to see here*
but I followed, at a distance,
to watch his tender wide waddle
cross the road to the pond
where his goose brethren gathered.

You need to stand with the sun at your back
to see anything clearly
but even then sometimes
the distance blurs.
I know how often I've seen
what I've wanted too.

And anyway, fog is tricky,
hiding mountains,
changing shape—each tiny droplet
has reflection, has shadow,
has a way of turning
everything gray.

Dog Walk

for Michelle

This is where we catch up our days:
her daughter pulsing into adolescence,
how loud I find the silence of my son,
also politics, ignorance—willful and otherwise—
her age-old distrust of religion, my re-found faith,
the patch of ocean garbage, that plastic glut
filling the belly of the baby albatross
thousands of miles away from here—the fires
and floods that hold up devastation
to scales we can't weigh—how we will, both, try
to take our children this very summer
to see glaciers in Montana because, before they are here,
near to our age now, there will be no glaciers there—
also gunshots, and children, the way this country
perpetuates freedom like an emptied ringing,
also moonshots and the boy I know
who came through cancer—the miracle
and reprieve of it always running like a current
alongside, a cliff you step off or back from, falling
maybe before naming that you are falling, before noticing
that you have—the dogs, her old red hound,
my young pup, follow their known path:
out of town, uphill, over the busy highway, to woods
becoming less and less wooded.
The habit so well worn that, now,
when one of us says, out loud, *I need a dog walk*—
the children, even the husbands, know.
The dogs take for granted
that this is, of course, how we hold
our lives between us,
each staring down their own front door,
waiting to be let out.

Octopus

after Sarah Wilson & Kay Redfield Jamison

To conquer a beast,
so the old Chinese proverb goes,
you must first make it beautiful—
offering latitude or space,
let's call it language, for naming
what ails and aches, what rattles clear through
the great gaping maw shifting shape
like something not human—
bleeds blue, beats three hearts
and thinks with feeling clear through the whole,
each arm—longing and loosening
the way it blends, changes skin
not just color but tone, texture, shape—
what is there to say, at the end then
when asked: who are you, what are you,
what did you desire? How to say
without speaking: I didn't know.
And what would it be to say: I danced
and spun and dove
in the ether
and didn't ever know
the limits
of my own skin.

Crepidula

I held it to the sun, checked,
and checked again, that it was only remnant:
a tight baby fist of a shell,
wound upon itself, whorls
of blood purple, burgundy—
seams like wrinkles—like lifelines—

Later, my son said he saw it open
into three parts. I only half believed.
His mind tilts and soars like a bird
able to bear heavy winds and still,
somehow, find landing—
but then I saw the shell open,
just as he said, a tiny accordion—

I rushed back to the beach,
whispered, *good luck,* and aimed
just past wave crash—
seagulls swarmed, angry or intent,
and I told myself it looked deep enough
for sinking.

Google said it was a stack of slipper shells,
invasive limpets fused and procreating,
shifting male to female in a lifetime—
and I marvel at assumptions,
how they beleaguer and undo us—
how often I fight myself to stillness
when my son is rambling
about Minecraft or magic tricks,
airplanes or all the ways to solve
a Rubix cube—
I gaze toward his cadence
sometimes without hearing anything

but how much I want him to survive—
to add his strange moving beauty
to this world, to sink or to rise,
to find or be found.

A Presbyterian Walks into a Crystal Shop

for Melina

My friend listens to stones,
says they choose her—*What do you want,*
she asks and I don't know—
I am distracted: rutilated quartz,
aquamarine, selenite, jasper, amethyst,
tiger eye—*What do you need?*
she asks as if I know.
I squint and bend and almost kneel
to read each worn-eared cardboard sign:
clarity, peace, prosperity, balance.
Eventually, I shrug my stone-filled hands.
She studies my clutch, bites her lip,
replaces one, then two—
This one's better, she says, adds tourmaline
and goldstone. *For protection,*
and strength, she says, sure of it.
Usually I just pray, I joke out loud
but even when I pray I half
imagine God's side-eye
for not doing it right—my dull thud
of *Dear Father* for solidity,
a place to start. Words like protect,
forgive, surround, heal—
all small and weighted,
tumble out my mouth into one day's end
and the next—
it's not that nothing is beautiful
or true—
just that so many things are:
all these crumbs
we hold too, all we try to gather—
our usual words
that sound like questions, or the answer

you pretend to hear
when a friend hands you a stone
lit through with stardust
and says it's just for you.

RON: Remain(ing) Overnight

I wake without knowing where:
crisp sheets, easily bleached
and the sheer light that speaks
of time zone and distance,
absence and presence. My shape
in the bed, my mind thick
with the day still clinging—
one hundred forty-three smiles,
at least, and so many ice cubes
and ginger ales, napkins and pretzels,
all the ways I've learned to say goodbye—
to look forward to a nowhere
that slightly resembles everywhere:
a wheeled walk from airplanes,
a van ride, a nest of pillows, a balcony
overlooking other balconies
or rooftops, or seagulls, sometimes
the sound of airplanes—
if the windows open
I open them, pull the sheer curtain
across to keep the light
and pretend I am unseen—
the way a body or a dress,
or a curtain might fall
or rise or even beckon
memory—how you are you
and you, too, are here,
lingering.

Great Blue

In the creek she is a stillness.
Sunlight outlines
the day's cold—the feathers
at her neck a shabby scarf,
clumps of leaves gather
and catch against legs so thin
that, at first, I only see sticks.

I try not to wonder
if that stillness is her trick,
how she stays uncaught,
how she holds off the big cats,
or the foxes—or the human
kind of cruelty that hurts
things just because.

There was one, once, down
by the bridge where we
used to stop to look for turtles
or frogs or water bugs—
when my sons were little
and always with me—
it took my eyes too long
to fasten and acknowledge
that it wasn't rope or rag
but feathers and bone.

This one blinks
and a part of me
wants to startle, see her
push up and open out
into the space of sky above us—
above me—an umbrella
that won't quite open.

The Story They Are Telling Now

The thwack—thwack—thwack of something breaking,
something falling
startled me this morning, brought me out,
my breath a cloud I stepped through,
as I pulled my bathrobe close and found you
lobbing an old brick at some frozen ice in our small yard.
I glanced toward the neighboring houses, snugged wall
to wall with ours, and wondered who you woke.
You have always thrown things,
forgetting you were indoors, forgetting
the fragility of glass, narrowly missing
your little brother's head, cringing if it hit your father,
or the dog. It served you well in Little League.
Even now nothing stays in your hands for very long—
as if you are still testing gravity, testing me
to see if I will stoop and pick things up—thwack—
"It doesn't break," you grinned at me, red cheeked,
so that I saw you, four or five years ago, peering out
from the length of you now—your hair a trademark shag,
your face taking on my father, and yours.
"I never would have thought to do that," I said
and knew it maybe wasn't true, I've just been told
a different story all my life about what there is to lose
and how often things can't go back
to what they were. I know the story they are telling now—
the one they've been telling you since you were born,
the same one they told your father
and your grandfather—isn't as true as they say.
You don't have to throw yourself against anything
to see if you will break.
I can tell you: you will.
Lately, I can't seem to find a way to tell you I understand.
It feels like flying
and falling, both.

The world is always becoming.
But it's also what it's always been.
And it matters what you break.

My Mother Never Listens to the Lyrics

I still sometimes get fooled
by a melody, a seamless burst
of brassy punctuation,
an upbeat rhythm of jaunt
that matches a gait, a flash
of smile—I know
the lyric tells itself—
but sing prettily enough
and no one will know
to listen as time topples
the lot of us, and those we love—
it's always there, that small clock
like a misshapen fist,
that lub dub lub dub lub dub
of our existence.
My mother might say it's easier
and good and kind
to put on a song
that sings jauntily
of jazz and strolling,
an exasperated sweetheart,
she implores me not to listen
to the undertone,
or the way our hearts
can't help but falter.

Bones

My shoulder popped hard last night
when I turned over in bed
the noise of it a solid sound
reverberating —
and my ankles on the stairs
in the early morning
should wake the children.

My bones seem to be
pronouncing their existence,
their hard tack
beneath my surface of soft —
I feel more and more the absence
of wings
either that I had them
once, but more
like I could have them,
can feel exactly where they might sprout
or bud,
blossom or grow —

I think it would hurt
and people would stare
but I marvel anyway
to feel the push of these bones
against the casing of this skin.

The Lungs Were So Named Because of Their Lightness

Looking too close at anything might prove
unbearable—all intimacy moves
need—essential, weight-bearing—all
gasp and grasp and exhale—

Look at leaves or maybe their absence, that
unction of nakedness come winter, that
narrowing, how we wait—holding
grief, or exaltation.

During Boarding, February 2020

At mid-cabin, I forgot
to say good morning
to the passenger, her face
split by a cartoon mask:
exaggerated red lips,
a beauty mole, and a pencil-thin
mustache with Dalian flare—

Sometimes the plane
feels like it's moving
when it's not, and there's always
a moment of disbelief
during takeoff—
that barrel down a runway,
that impossible lift—

Sometimes midflight, mid
conversation
I lose the thread—
find myself blinking—
naked like a mole rat
set sudden into light
or foiled at a dead end
of stone—

the masked woman spoke
good morning to me
as if everything were normal
but I was already seasick
saw the future
in an instant—remember?

This was before.

When the Sky Tips

I force him out each day, my child,
not yet twelve, somewhere in the blur
between log on, assignments due
and our skinny house with his big brother
suddenly the size of a man, his father home
all the time—and all his friends behind a screen.
We wander out the same path,
toward a neighborhood with trees
that are old, with houses alone
and surrounded by yard.
I collapse my eyes enough to see
just the treetops twining
just his small face astonished
by its own self reflecting,
caught between that flight of being,
seeing clear to how to uphold
and bend, knowing
what burdens we bear
to keep us tethered. He takes my hand
tells me to look up
keep looking
as if there is a central point,
a gathering energy,
his, maybe, swollen from me,
formed and hovering—
just as I am, just as we all are
when the sky tips
and the birds lift up
and our eyes follow
trees wandering—
or is it wondering—
sky.

Banana Bread

How often have I tried a thing
only to find it's not as they say.
There are things needed
that I didn't know or understand,
my frame of reference differing
from theirs, from everyone's apparently
as all the likes and shares attest,
all the comments: *Great recipe! So easy! Yumm!!*
And me: the edges burn, the center
sinks, the middle gooey and wet
and it never ever comes out clean
from the pan—I don't even like
banana bread. I just hate wasting
the bananas, hate wasting
anything, don't know what I'll have to say
for myself, years from now
when a child belonging to my son
or my son's son
asks me what it was like
to take a warm shower every day
to buy bread or fruit when I wanted it
without thought, without need,
throwing scraps off the deck
to the sparrows or making inedible
fruit bread—what will I say
when they ask what it was like
to live knowing
you were on the precipice
of time unsung—or, rather, end time
singing—the timer going off
and going off, an alarm
so long and ceaseless
that we didn't hear it anymore—we chose not
to hear it, our ears tuned out
the constant.

Underlying Conditions

It won't be weeks, but days, her doctor said.
My mother can't quite fathom
why—when I hear her restlessness,
when she says she's sure she'll be fine—
I insist on reminding her
how her body holds
susceptibility like side effects:
diabetes, asthma, age.
She says I always think of darkness.
Still, I ask my sons to call each day,
to play violin or piano
for her. I send puzzles,
masks, hand sanitizer.
And I beg her to stay home,
please, stay home—
because even if we don't stop to sleep,
even if we just make the kids peanut butter
sandwiches while the car is moving,
even taking the interstate straight from Virginia
up through Ohio, through all that grain:
Indiana, Nebraska, Wyoming—coming straight across—
it's still on, and on, and mountains
between here and home. Each day, I call
at the same time,
her morning, my noon.
I tell her how spring seems less riotous
this year, holding time and place
with its scheduled blooming.
But, just yesterday, maybe today,
I thought it was snowing
and it was just the serviceberry tree,
letting blossoms go.

Rare Sighting

There are so many birds this year,
my husband says, as if this is his first time
out in the world with his eyes open.
He tries every year with tomatoes.
I gave up when the kids were still small.
He nods his head toward a robin-sized bird,
gray and quick—*what's that one?*
A catbird, I say and know he doesn't quite believe me.
I've never seen one. Are you sure?
The bird perches on the brown paper edge
of the yard waste bag—almost manages it.
He's not afraid, my husband says
and repeats, *I've never seen one before.*
He expects they are rare—
and I don't say darling, you need
to get out more, or even, dearest, you should walk
with me an evening or two—
you do not always have to be so efficient
or alone. You want to give our sons
the whole of what you didn't have
but I could show you, I could name for you
some few familiar things: the company I've kept
while they've been growing
and you've been striving. Here
is the catbird, a mimic,
he sits, tail down, shoulders slightly hunched,
wings dangling a bit like the arms of someone
who doesn't know what he's looking at—
watching, and wanting, too, to know.

To My Father Whose Pitch Has Always Been About Surviving

Years and years you tried
to teach me.
Now, I call home
to remind you of fragility—
as if I can protect you
from one thing
and, so, everything,
keeping mom, keeping you
alive and we know enough
to not ask *until what*?
The distance between us
collapsed by a phone line.
The world pitches variants,
firestorms, floods.
We go slowly toward
forgetting and forgetting and forgetting.
Now I am the reminder,
the pitch of my voice
often off or too high,
filled as it is with too much
gathering behind it—

Sometime in the Late Age of a Long Marriage

When she's sleeping hard, my father
covers my mother's face with his hand,
just to make sure she's still breathing—like a person
searching out their glasses
in the middle of the night.
Meanwhile, my mother says, *I can't breathe.*
But she knows it ages him, the worry,
the way she sometimes doesn't wake,
blood sugar diving too low, too fast
for her to catch it—they both know
how a night might turn itself
inside out—how she might wake
to him angry and afraid, her sick
to her stomach—he should call for help
but he knows she won't forgive
the harsh light of an emergency room,
the way the doctor's eyes vague
past her, seeing only age, seeing only weight,
seeing only another diabetic
in America.
My father can't quite name
how he only sees her
as he did before—the girl
with the smile that offered
him the kind of life
he didn't think was his to claim.
He does what he can,
sleeps on the surface
of his dreaming, flailing
like a man about to drown
or maybe the way a boy breaks
the surface of water—all splash
and summer sunlight—
what is love for
if not to make sure
you're still breathing.

We Were Never Made to Be Invincible

As a child, my childish heart loved Robin Hood—
the cartoon version where he and Maid Marian
are foxes and when he runs the jailbreak
I loved most the little baby bunny
saying *mommy, mommy wait for me*
with her little bunny lisp in her little pink nightgown
trailing her little stuffed bunny—her mother
screamed *my baby* and Robin Hood turned back to look—
I loved how his face faltered—and determined,
in the same moment, to go back—the mother reaching
her arms out from the careening wagon—
I didn't even know then what it meant,
the bones and muscles involved,
the mother's heart behind it.
The world—my world—hadn't told me yet,
that there's always someone left behind,
or that to carry so much
for someone else was deemed a cost
too high to exact.
I know now that most of us would have kept going,
shook our heads and told the mother
there was nothing we could have done,
or, there was a war on, and we couldn't risk
a bigger one—or, we were frightened, we didn't mean
to shoot—but maybe I already knew
there was always grief to live beside and name.
Terrible destruction, surely, and terrible death—
the mourning can take you up on its back
and carry you—so that you wake not knowing
the how of the why
or even, for a moment, the where.
Flesh collapses so surely.
When morning comes—that sunlight—
what will be asked of us?

In Between

I could measure time to my father,
how his hand held mine,
how the phone is hard for us
because we both know how to do—
how the doing
is what holds the whole—

I see him in my son, his hands,
that crash and tangle
of genes—when Covid hit
the miles expanded, overnight—
and I said, *your Papa gets so restless,
maybe you could call him.*

Love can feel like a collision
in between a taut string,
at either end the surprise
of how they need
each other—my teen,
at 14, 15, 16—still calls
each night. My father
and my son, within reach
of all they might not ever say
to me.

Commute

My headlights on Route 15
at 3 am cut through the dark—
so thick it's pressing. A fog
rises over fields I cannot see
and sometimes the car alerts its light
on the side mirror—nothing's there
but maybe old ghosts hover.
What doesn't come out at night
in that wash of dark, and quiet?
This is Civil War country,
and, before that, the land my ancestors
took when we sought out ideas
of freedom. This soil
knows blood and the mists
feel familiar. A child with poor vision,
I could see form and shape
so clearly in a dark room—
shadows moved within shadows—
something upright, something sloppy,
that lurk and wait—I feared
consumption, feared the fall
into another world and often ran
or groped for light, my hand a panic—
the light a dissipation,
like a prayer. The parameter
of this car—its steel and glass,
the buzz of the radio, the heat
flaring, and me, soft lit
by the dash—I've learned
to keep my own company,
to stay awake, and lean
to watch for deer or possum
or fox tail—I am suspended
when I cross the bridge,
over the Potomac, between two states,
transient and caught.

Watching Mountains

Even though the room faces west,
the sunset plays the mountains,
and I see how long a day can be
well spent, standing still
and held there — two white birds
flicker with sunlight — the sky
as if it might snow, that mist of fog,
but then a late gasp of wide blue.
I am in the city at the base
of those mountains, a stretch
of the Rockies, caught between
time zones, between here
and back again. I stand
at a hotel window
naming want — those hills,
I mean, to be in them —
what is time to a mountain,
beyond season, beyond sun —
the gathering of rain —
a mountain lion's call,
the stone ringing with light
like a name that's learned to speak
for itself — what is it to feel yourself unmoving?
Any shift would rumble
like bone crack
like cadence, the fall of rock
or impact — they rest
the way the sea sways,
that wash of crash and pull.
There is no pulse
in a mountain — just the fact
of its being — as if to say here,
just here — a reminder
of what was, what is,
and someday immeasurable
what will no more be.

On Becoming the Type of Person Who Yells: Dinner!

Some things between us become habits
even after the feeling that began
them lifts or squanders itself
in daylight, that rinse
of time, sun after moon—
there is as much we can't ever say
and I think you are tired
of me trying to say it.
But the choice for me isn't one—
the way the crow, yesterday, focused
on her task of eating,
stopped to call back
to her brethren in the far trees—
swelling her throat,
aiming vibration
skyward, and slightly east,
trying all the while still to nourish herself
on something found
in the grass, something
at her feet—
our son says, *can you just not?*
and I don't know that I can
or can't. There is so much
we can't know
about the creatures we live beside,
no matter how we feed
each other, or what we call
from one level of our tall and narrow house
to the next—you grumbling
about needing to be on the same level,
saying you refuse to holler
from the basement to the kitchen
or the kitchen to the bedrooms
and me, hollering anyway—

caught as I am
between all there is to do,
all the ways I love,
all the ways I could disappear—
and how hard I'm trying not to.

Tammi Calls From Walmart

She must have her headphones on,
I can hear the background music
and other shoppers and her cart
with a bad wheel that rattles
and follows her through the aisles —
maybe vegetables, or frozen dinners,
easy to cook — soon, eventually,
all her husband will be able to eat
is mashed potatoes or Mac & Cheese.
I listen to her doing the things we do
and call living — dish soap, maybe socks —
surely alcohol. We talk like we are good
at ice skating — straight sentences push us along,
evenly, or accidentally aim us
right at her husband's ALS diagnosis at 53.
I can't even believe what's normal now,
she says and we are through — wet, struggling —
our street clothes pulling us down — our hair plastered
to our middle-aged faces and I have to try
to fish her out, make a joke as I pull and tug
her back to Walmart, to the cart
with the wonky wheel, my only tool
my voice and decades of story
between us. Of course, all loss is speakable
if you learn — or remember — how to surface.
Blue sky or cloudy, it doesn't matter which, not really,
just that it's still there, holding,
for now — and anyway you need groceries,
dinner, someone has to mow the lawn,
wash the car, tell the kids.
I don't know how but I'm doing it,
she says, from self-checkout,
scanning erratic beeps
and I know I'm a hindrance now,

say, I'll call again soon, feel that woozy sense
I've known so often lately like a thin place,
maybe the top of a mountain—the air there,
the view, and all around me scattershot
of boulder, cloud and tree—

I Broke the Way Land Breaks

My son asks if I ever feel bad
for inanimate objects
and I think of his Nana's house,
or ours—his own room
glutted with junk and treasure,
and I wonder—no, I know—
he will hold on too long
to many things
and fight his whole life to name
what is missing.
The world is so big, buddy,
I want to say—some things
get a little lost.
Even eating dinner, he paces,
pops up and down,
that mind a ricochet—his brother and dad and I
numb on screen time.
Sure, sometimes I shake my head like a horse
buzzed by something it cannot name
besides the buzzing—
these pandemic years have worn me
like a sock
with a sudden hole,
the floor cold and my skin
pushing through. I have wandered
through all this trying
and forgot, forget
how to name space for what is here.
It's not all my fault. The world
is wild with terror and teeth,
with weeping—and I am weaker
than I expected. I broke
the way land breaks—
my soil, stone, and sun cracked

by too much at once.
Whether she said it or not,
I remember my mother asking
me to not be so hard.
I looked elsewhere, then, too—
propelled out, seeking
heat, seeking rain
and light—the whole storm.
Kiddo, I should tell him, kiddo,
it's easy to confuse
what we love—what we need
to love—what needs
our love. We are only creature,
near enough animal,
near enough plant,
near enough
gone.

I Have Had to Remind Myself to Breathe for Years Now

Watch the lit moon through cloud swift
and you'll know what I mean
when I say there is much to hold
or raise up or even name,
at least for a minute, as mine.
I have never been able to pretend
there isn't loss, or that it isn't hard,
because time is loss and gumption,
the dare of a doing or not —
the choice made, and given,
the noise it renders through
and of me — I mean sea
song, and still mountains.
I mean the way a boy
becomes tall and how his hugs
stay awkward for so long —
where to put the arms now, the hands —
how to hold a thing that's shifting,
fast, and flickering away — think of birds
their rush of breath and heartbeat,
wingspan and the hover —
how an illness or injury can stay
you, hold you captive
to new measures — fear trembles
clear through to new knowing —
I mean it's all so close,
almost always, any possibility,
and I have had to remind myself
to breathe for years now
because I can't carry everyone
I love across the line
where they might need carrying —
I've tried and I can't always see the line
even in the trying. I've learned

the trees hold the seasons, but also patience—
that surrender—how to wait and let
the sky be, the clouds and rain
and sunlight, how to bud
and blossom, from viridescent
to full viridian, to that beauty
that holds as it is faltering,
fall colors like a gasp, an exhale
and then, almost always,
without fail, the letting go.

Raising Glaciers

If you look you can trace
the path of us. Measure snow pack
with your eyes: before, and before, and now
streams weep down mountain waterfalls,
the face of stone scarred and pocked
and jagged—no change goes smoothly.
I have been trying to show my sons
how to name—loss—and is it betrayal
to give them such language
in a world shifting toward flashpoint
and heat? What else is it
to be human—I run out of words
to answer their gaze,
drive them to mountains,
give them landscape, offer
this disappearing world
as if it is one long gasp
of oh and awe, and see—do you see?
I am raising glaciers—
lost causes, boys
with too soft hearts who know not to take
stones or approach wildlife, who know
how to name what is here, what is lost
if we can't name it.
Maybe the earth knows
the sun is too much—
and, anyway, catches
all the light it can.

In 2022, Rebecca Brock won *The Comstock Review's* Muriel Craft Bailey Memorial Poetry Contest, the Kelsay Women's Poetry Contest and *Sheila-Na-Gig online's* Editor's Choice Award. Her work has been recognized and honored by *Cutthroat: A Journal of the Arts, River Heron Review,* and *Whale Road Review.* Her chapbook, *Each Bearing Out* (Kelsay Books 2022) was a semifinalist in the 2021 New Women's Voices contest at Finishing Line Press. She holds an MFA in fiction from Bennington College. Her nonfiction essay about being a working flight attendant on 9/11 was published in the *Threepenny Review* and earned a Pushcart Honorable Mention. She has been a flight attendant for most of her adult life and is still surprised by this fact. Idaho born, she lives in Virginia with her family but takes them westward as often as she can. You can find more of her work at RebeccaBrock.org.

Sheila-Na-Gig Editions

www.ingramcontent.com/pod-product-compliance
Lightning Source LLC
Chambersburg PA
CBHW020330130626
46549CB00003B/1100